The changing face of Britain's favc

BLACKPOOL

THEN & NOW

By Craig Fleming and Steve Singleton

A special souvenir publication brought to you by

The Gazette

and

at heart ♡ publications

Acknowledgements

A book of this sort can only be researched, compiled and written with the co-operation of many people.

Particular thanks go to the generations of *Gazette* photographers for preserving this historical record and to chief librarian Carole Davies for hours of painstaking searching through the archives. In addition thanks go to Ted Lightbown chairman of the Blackpool and Fylde Historical Society and Barry Shaw, president of the Blackpool Civic Trust.

First Published in 2007 by:
The Blackpool Gazette,
in conjunction with
At Heart Ltd, 32 Stamford Street, Altrincham,
Cheshire, WA14 1EY.

Printed and bound by Bell & Bain Ltd., Glasgow

ISBN: 978-1-84547-153-8

INTRODUCTION

UNCOVER the changing face of Blackpool....

Having started life as little more than a few fishermen's cottages, Blackpool quickly became a magnet for young and old alike.

The Northern mill workers were among the first to pack trains and charabancs in their annual search for seaside fun, to sample the blossoming resort's unique atmosphere and bracing sea breezes.

Many millions followed from all over the country and they helped make Blackpool what it is today – Britain's number one holiday resort with a rich entertainment heritage – and constantly changing.

Most of the development has been in the 20th century, coinciding with the growth in the tourism industry. But the builders were not only concerned with creating promenade attractions, seafront hotels and guesthouses.

Much of the residential property was built between the wars and in the space of just 200 years, Blackpool grew into one of the most densely populated urban areas outside London.

With this in mind *The Gazette* has gone back in time to reveal the resort from its early roots to the present day.

Many of the properties here have previously appeared in *The Gazette's* popular 'Then and Now' feature in our weekly Memory Lane pages every Tuesday and Saturday. Others come from our extensive archives, while some are rare, contributed photographs.

With *The Gazette's* own photographers having revisited familiar landmarks and favourite corners of the town, it is clear some are almost identical to how they appeared in those 'good old days' while others have since changed beyond all recognition.

Blackpool can be proud of its work in protecting top cultural buildings, while many new buildings have emerged and historic landmarks have been retained.

This is a fascinating collection of photographs – to form a lasting souvenir of the seaside resort's history.

Delve inside to see how Blackpool was then – and is now!

Steve Singleton
The Gazette

Victoria Street

One of the main roads in the heart of the town centre is Victoria Street pictured here in 1860.

In the background is Bank Hey House – the home of William Cocker – where the familiar Winter Gardens archway can now be seen at the end of the street. Part of the 1846 Cocker home survives inside the Winter Gardens today.

People were still living in cottages in what is now Blackpool's shopping centre in the 1920s and 30s. Some were demolished when *The*

Gazette and Herald expanded its original town centre offices

The biggest changes to Victoria Street came in October 1977 when work began on Blackpool's £5 million covered shopping complex The Hounds Hill Centre. The shopping centre, named after a long-lost district of the resort, was bounded by Victoria Street, Adelaide Street, Tower Street and the rear of properties fronting Bank Hey Street.

The Manchester

Ask any regular visitor where The Manchester is and the chances are they'll quickly direct you just south of Central Pier on Blackpool Promenade.

Most will realise that you mean the Manchester Hotel, one of the biggest pubs in the resort. It was once the first port of call for many a party arriving at the Coliseum coach station in nearby Tyldesley Road. But as our pictures show there have been several Manchester buildings on the same site at the junction of

Lytham Road and the seafront – commonly known as Manchester Square.

Oldest of our photographs dates from 1860, when it was Hemingway's Manchester Hotel, later becoming part of the C & S Brewery estate.

That company demolished and rebuilt the pub which was there from 1936, surviving 60 years with various internal and external facelifts.

Brewer Bass was forced to rebuild the pub because the building's steel frame

was becoming corroded. This move angered local historians who felt the classic piece of 1930s Art Deco should have been listed. But the building's fate was decided when the Department of National Heritage turned down an application for listed status and the current red brick version opened in May 1996.

Oxford Square

Great Marton Windmill is long gone, but the building alongside, at the Oxford Square end of Waterloo Road, remains – albeit with a different name.

The mill was built in the 1700s and in 1775, James Willacy was the miller, living in a nearby brick cottage.

In 1876, a consortium led by William Flitcroft, a cotton waste dealer from Preston, bought the mill, cottages and other buildings. All but the mill were replaced by The Oxford Hotel, which

also boasted pleasure gardens and a bowling green.

The mill was demolished in December 1900 and what was Mill Lane eventually became part of Waterloo Road.

The watering hole is there today, but was recently rebranded as Bickerstaffes – itself a name forever linked with Blackpool's heritage.

Central Beach

Look out to sea from this section of Blackpool Promenade and the view will be the same today as it was in 1878.

But look at the land from the identical point on the sands and what you see is worlds apart.

In the earlier photograph, the Palatine Hotel, at the very right with its distinctive turret, stood on the Promenade corner of Hounds Hill.

In the name of progress it was demolished in the mid 1970s to make way for a structure that is very much of its time. The Palatine

Buildings houses several stores at ground level and over the years there have been various nightspots in the basement and upper floors.

To the left of the new picture, at Adelaide Place, is the distinctive 1930s building complete with clock tower, still a landmark alongside Blackpool Tower. Created originally as a prestigious seafront store for Woolworths – who have since moved a couple of blocks further up the Promenade – it is now home to Pricebusters.

The older photograph shows the block that housed the Royal Hotel before demolition and, in the distance, is the old Central Methodist Church, another victim of 1970s redevelopment, although a new church was created above a block of shops.

South King Street

Hello, hello, hello, what's all this then? Blackpool bobbies are soon to be on the move again as grand designs unfold for the Golden Mile.

The high-rise fortress on Bonny Street, home to the police since the early 1970s, will be demolished to make way for the proposed conference and casino buildings.

The thin blue line has grown thicker since the middle of the 19th century when Blackpool was policed by just one constable, named Banks of the Lancashire Constabulary.

Following police stations built, firstly in Bonny Street and later in Abingdon Street, the Blackpool Borough Police Force was formed in 1887.

J C Derham was appointed first Chief Constable and had a full complement of 20. By 1893 it was decided the Abingdon Street station was inadequate and on June 5 of that year, the South King Street premises (pictured left) were opened. According to the Chief Constable's report of 1893: "Thirty two males and 16 females were dealt with on charges of larcency. Four were under the age of 15. Three were whipped and one sent to reformatory school".

The South King Street premises were later demolished to be replaced by council offices and Blackpool Register Office.

Blackpool Tower

The most famous of Blackpool's landmarks is of course the Tower, which opened at Whitsuntide 1894 – complete with circus and ballroom. It mirrored the success of the Eiffel Tower in Paris, completed in 1899, which had led to a rash of tower projects in the UK although many never got off the ground.

One that did was at New Brighton on the Mersey but Blackpool's was the big success. The project was led by Alderman Sir John Bickerstaffe who, from humble beginnings as a fisherman's son, went on to become Mayor of the town and an honorary Freeman of the Borough.

The Tower was built by Heenan and Froude, based at Newton Heath, Manchester, and commemorative medals were struck to mark the laying of the foundation stone in 1891.

An army of intrepid workers, known as stick men, had the unenviable task of painting the 518 foot tower to protect it from the elements. The Tower frontage has regularly been updated to keep pace with modern trends.

In 1984 the Tower received Grade 1 listed building status and a restoration programme revealed once again murals, tiles and walls which had been covered since 1977.

St John's Church

This building has been a focal point in Blackpool town centre in three separate centuries.

The original St John's Church was consecrated by the Bishop of Chester in July 1821 and completed in 1824 at a cost of £1,070 0s 5d, the money coming from leading local figures and the public.

As Blackpool grew it was decided that a larger church was needed and in 1877 the building was demolished, with the new church construction starting immediately.

Blackpool Mayor Dr W H Cocker, who donated £1,000 to the new church fund, laid the foundation stone and the

church was completed in 1878.

It is viewed, in the first of our two pictures, in the 1890s, from what was Cedar Street. In 1924 the corporation found it again necessary to widen the junction of Church Street and Abingdon Street and this necessitated the removal of a number of bodies from the church graveyard.

As part of the agreement with the church, the corporation undertook to lay the churchyard as open space forever. In more recent times, huge internal and external changes at St John's have saved it from demolition as the infrastructure was crumbling.

In March 2006, a six year makeover culminated in a service of re-dedication, confirming St John's the Evangelist in the heart of Blackpool as the Parish and Civic Church of the resort.

Changes to the church include extensive internal development to create a new community and conference centre, a contemporary worship area and restoration of the chapel.

A heritage centre has been created, along with new separate community and church entrances, and Blackpool's "other" Tower has been totally renovated.

Central Beach

Seven miles of unspoilt sand proved a magnet for tens of thousands of Northern mill workers who helped make Blackpool what it is today – Britain's premier resort.

They came in their droves to sample its unique atmosphere and bracing seas breezes. Central Beach was a sea of humanity with bathing huts and sailboats, donkeys, swings, Punch and Judy and traders selling all manner of items including jugs of tea.

Although there are many alternative pursuits away from the prom today, when the sun shines the beach

remains just as much the
natural, ageless crowd
pulling attraction for
thousands of holidaymakers
and day-trippers

Uncle Tom's Cabin

Uncle Tom's Cabin was a pioneer of Blackpool's entertainment industry and became the resort's first and most popular landmark for over half a century.

The original venue evolved in 1851 when Margaret Parkinson set up a refreshment stall selling gingerbread and ginger beer to visitors walking along the cliff tops on Blackpool's northern shores.

In the late 1850s a cabin was added and taken over by Robert Taylor and William A Parker who continued the thriving business.

Over the years they introduced other attractions including a dancing pavilion, a concert hall (complete with music hall artistes and burlesque turns), a

photographic studio and camera obscura.

Following the introduction of a liquor, spirits and alcohol licence, visitors flocked to Uncle Tom's in their thousands. The name Uncle Tom refers to Margaret Parkinson's brother-in-law, farmer Thomas Parkinson, who owned the land and whom her son referred to as Uncle Tom.

To further promote the cabin, three wooden figures were erected representing the characters Uncle Tom, Little Eva and Topsy, from Harriet Beecher Stowe's novel *Uncle Tom's Cabin* published in 1852.

Sadly, in 1907, Uncle Tom's was taken down after part of the building collapsed into the sea because of erosion of the cliffs. Today the site is occupied by the lift overlooking North Shore Boating Pool.

A new Uncle Tom's Cabin opened that same year on the opposite side on what is now Queens Promenade and the licence was transferred.

A century on, this "new" Uncle Tom's Cabin remains a popular watering hole – with entertainment – for both visitors and locals alike.

South Promenade

What's the connection between a man of the cloth, an ice cream cone and a chocolate flake? The answer lies in a building at the north corner of South Promenade and Station Road.

The first church in South Shore opened in 1837 and was dedicated to the Holy Trinity and the original vicar was the Rev J F Green.

His home overlooked the sea and the vicarage later became Pablo's ice cream parlour and café – a role that it retains today.

The neighbouring property is also still part of the seafront scene although, as our second photograph shows, it has long since lost its imposing bay windows, chimney pots and other trappings. And the visitors are in shorter supply too although the same pavement is guaranteed to be deep in pedestrians on busy Illuminations Saturdays.

New House Farm

By the turn of the 1900s 'the march of progress' – Blackpool's motto – was certainly on. Yet the rural community was still thriving, if you strayed far enough away from the seafront. There were numerous whitewashed farms and cobbled walls. This is New House Farm, with its corrugated roof, which stood at the corner of Snow Lane, later renamed Cherry Tree Road, Marton. The farm was 300 years old when it was demolished in 1929 for the widening of

Preston New Road. The farm site was later occupied by The Telefusion building which was purchased and refitted to become *The Evening Gazette* offices in 1987, officially opened by then Home Secretary Douglas Hurd.

Ten years later *The Gazette* moved out and the bulldozers moved in to create today's Kentucky Fried Chicken restaurant and drive-thru.

Talbot Square

One of Blackpool's most historic areas, Talbot Square, which is at the heart of the town centre conservation area and houses the "new" Town Hall completed in 1900 and Yates' Wine Lodge, built as the Theatre Royal in 1868.

Around £2.25m is to be spent on buildings in Talbot Road, Clifton Street and Abingdon Street as part of the Townscape heritage initiative. Vacant floorspace will be brought back into use, lost architectural features will be re-instated

and open spaces will get a
makeover.

In the 1910 summer
scene the square is full of
hustle and bustle as people
queue to board trams. In
contrast the present day
view looks less crowded.

Topping Street

When this first photograph was taken back in 1904, parking meters had yet to rear their ugly pay slots.

It was near the edge of town with only the occasional shop between the railing-lined house frontages.

Over the rooftops to the left is the sign on the roof of the Hippodrome Theatre in Church Street – previously the Empire and these days remodelled after years as a cinema into the Syndicate nightclub.

As can be seen in the

newer photograph, the signs
along Topping Street are
more likely to be
highlighting take away food
outlets, chip shops and
restaurants.

Central Drive

This 1906 view of Central Drive is not so different today.

To the left, over the wall, were the railway sidings of Central Station.

Now a car park, all that remains from the glory days of steam is the block of public toilets which for BBC comedy drama Viva Blackpool was transformed into a much more glamorous Vegas-style Chapel of Love!

To the right of the photograph is a jewellers and fancy goods shop at the junction with Hornby Road, now an off-licence.

The Tower still rises from above the roofs, of course, joined by the occasional loft space bedroom.

But there are no gas lamps and the tramway route up Central Drive to Waterloo Road, which opened in 1902, was little more than a memory after 1936.

This now busy road was

previously named Great Marton Road and, further south Grasmere Road was known as Central Road.

North and Central Station

Once the gateways to Blackpool for generations of holidaymakers, neither North nor Central Railway Station buildings remain today.

In its heyday, Central (top right), which opened in 1863 as part of the Blackpool and Lytham Railway, would deliver thousands of visitors at a time into Hounds Hill and onto the Promenade.

The station was given a new facade in 1899, but 1964 saw the Beeching axe fall. The station and the line to South Shore closed and

the site became another gateway – this time the far end of Europe's largest car park with spaces for a staggering 3,755 vehicles! The terminus itself was demolished in the early 1970s and replaced (centre right) by the Coral Island amusement complex, officially opened by comedian Ken Dodd. The building in the background, once a Marks and Spencer store, now houses several stores and a fast food restaurant. The old Lancashire, Yorkshire, London and North Western Railway companies originally ran North Shore station (pictured left) when it opened in 1898. This grand building at the corner of Talbot Road and Dickson Road, pictured in 1907, was demolished in 1974 in favour of a retail store (bottom right).

The present Blackpool North terminus was opened on the site of the old excursion platforms at the rear and now there are bold plans for the revitalisation of the Talbot Gateway with an integrated transport hub.

Promenade and Shaw Road

Corner scenes just over 100 years apart. At the turn of the century, the junction of the Promenade and Shaw Road boasted a busy-looking shop and office.

It sold toys and fancy goods and was also the office of Teddy Ashton's *Northern Weekly*. Teddy Ashton was one of the pseudonyms used by well-known writer, novelist, local historian and sociologist Allen Clarke (1863-1935). He can be seen in the earlier photograph talking to the children. Allen also wrote a

book *Effects on the Factory System*, translated into many languages, the Russian edition being prefaced by Tolstoy. Allen is best remembered for his Windmill Land series of books, the first of which was published in 1916.

Neighbouring properties remain, but today the corner block has been replaced with a fish and chip restaurant and takeaway.

The Opera House

The Opera House seen from Abingdon Street in 1908 with the original arched entrance to the Empress Ballroom in the centre of the Empress Buildings on Church Street.

The Winter Gardens with open air gardens and skating rink was formally opened in July 1878 and enjoyed mixed fortunes until the Opera House, then known as Her Majesty's was added in 1889, having been designed by Frank Matcham.

The present Opera House is the third on the

same site and was designed by Blackpool architect Charles MacKeith. It was the largest theatre in the country, seating almost 3,000 people, when it opened in 1939 with the biggest stage in Britain.

The theatre had the honour of staging the first Royal Variety Show outside London, in 1955, when the Queen and Duke of Edinburgh watched from the specially built Royal Box.

North Pier

North Pier has been an integral part of Blackpool's entertainment scene for almost 150 years.

Blackpool's first – and longest – pier was opened in 1863 and was designed to seat between 3,000 and 4,000 people at a time. Such was its popularity that half a million patrons passed through its promenade gates in its first year.

The jetty was added in 1869 and, in 1874, a further acre of decking was added on the Pier's north side to accommodate the Indian Pavilion while an open-air

bandstand was added on the south side.

As well as affording "greater promenading space of the most invigorating kind" the pier also welcomed pleasure boats which made regular sailings to Southport, Barrow and Piel island.

Serious fires destroyed the Indian Pavilion in both 1921 and 1938 but a new Art Deco pavilion rose from the ashes in 1939 to become one of the resort's most popular venues for summer show stars.

Fire was again to strike the pier frontage in 1966,

not longer after the wraps came off a major redevelopment scheme, but the crowds kept on coming and on a typical summer's day in the sixties the length of the pier would be crammed with deckchairs – with not an empty seat in sight.

Corporation Street

Older readers may remember St John's Market in Blackpool.

Not the one demolished in recent years at the side of Talbot Road bus station, but rather the bustling affair which operated from the town centre between 1893 and 1938.

After the market was demolished, Euston Street, which was cobbled, disappeared so that the site could be extended to build British Home Stores and adjoining shops topped by the West Street multi-storey car park. Both photographs are taken from the junction

of Corporation Street and
Birley Street.

Devonshire Road School

Risen from the ashes, that's Devonshire Primary School, which began a new lease of life in 2006.

A £7 million state-of-the-art building opened its doors to 450 pupils after the old premises were destroyed in an arson attack by children in August 2003.

Devonshire Road Council School opened on the corner of Devonshire Road and Caunce Street, Blackpool, in 1903 with 730 pupils, under the control of Mr J. P. Ogden.

The foundation stone bore the Blackpool School Board name but the boards were abolished by the 1902 Education Act and the Blackpool Education Committee took responsibility for the school.

In 1911, when the older of the two pictures was taken, the Devonshire Road Junior School, with provision for 500 children, had opened alongside.

The three R's were taught with history, geography, humanities, woodwork for boys, cookery for girls, games and music.

In the older photograph youngsters are playing in the yard and you can also see the cobbles being set into the road at what is now a busy junction.

St Nicholas School

St Nicholas School, Marton Moss, originally combined with the church, was opened and celebrated by a public tea party on Easter Wednesday, April 16, 1873.

It replaced the small Dame School, then in Division Lane. The school was described as being "a monument of generosity" by the Clifton family, of Lytham Hall.

Built in a very rural Marton Moss, on School Road the early school log book relates to pupils being absent, especially at potato planting, haymaking and harvesting times.

Over the years the school has been extended, mainly in 1927, when the headmaster's accommodation – seen in the earlier photograph covered in ivy – was taken down to make way for this major extension in a similar style to the section it replaced.

The original 1873 part of the school can be seen in the background of the photograph taken around 1910. Headmaster Anthony Hargreaves, at the school from 1905 to 1921, is pictured with staff and pupils, some spilling out onto the road, oblivious to

any horse drawn or other traffic. The second picture shows the present school staff and pupils of classes three and five. All the pupils are safely behind the railings on a road that has got increasingly busier in the 90 year gap between pictures.

Pleasure Beach Casino

Here's a glimpse of Blackpool's "casino" past. The oldest of these three images dates back to around 1913 when one of the resort's earliest cinemas opened in the ornate Casino building at the Pleasure Beach.

In addition to the 700 seater cinema, the building contained a billiard hall, restaurant and company offices.

In the early years it operated much like other cinemas of the day. Then, in 1934 it became a novelty

cinema, showing newsreels, cartoons and general interest films.

Despite its name, gambling was not allowed and, in 1939, the original Casino made way for the present Grade II listed Art Deco circular casino, designed by architect Joseph Emberton.

But the style of the old building lives on, the design used as the facade of the Coasters bar and restaurant at the southern end of the fun park's Ocean Boulevard.

Layton Square

This is one square changed in appearance by a roundabout.

The distinctive tram shelter, used by thousands of travellers to and from Blackpool seafront, is long gone, replaced by the roundabout that is a feature of busy Layton Square.

The first photograph was taken in 1914.

It shows the tram shelter and terminus of the tram road line from Talbot Square. To the right is the original Salem Methodist Iron Church.

The present building,
seen in the new photograph,
was opened in 1939 on
Westcliffe Drive that is now
a dual carriageway.

Moore Street

It's a much changed view at this South Shore junction where Rawcliffe Street crosses Moore Street.

To the left, back in 1915, was Ebeneezer Chapel Wesleyan Methodist Church which could seat 670. To the right were its Sunday Schools.

The Blackpool Times and *Fylde Coast Observer* newspaper of March 27, 1915, reported that the school was the venue for the speech night for Blackpool

High School, South Shore, when the headmaster presented his annual report, books and certificates were handed out and there was entertainment by pupils.

The church buildings on either side of Moore Street are now demolished and, as can be seen in the newer picture, have been replaced by blocks of flats.

In the distance, Moore Street crosses busy Waterloo Road with its modern shop block, right through to St Bede's Avenue, where the three storey properties still welcome their holiday guests.

Devonshire Square

Devonshire Square is one of Blackpool's busiest junctions, but when the first of these two photographs was taken in the 1920s cars were probably no more frequent than trams trundling through.

In the centre of the square was the rustic style combined sub station and tram shelter, clearly visible in the older photograph.

On the right, on the corner with Newton Drive, is the old Number Three and Didsbury Hotel. The tree lined roads were a council

initiative to add some relief and greenery to the increasingly built-up areas of Blackpool.

The new photograph, shows that most of these trees have now been felled. The long-hidden tram tracks have been replaced by white traffic lines.

A more modern substation remains at the heart of the square, alongside what has become a growing number of disused public toilets, while the Number Three pub now boasts a beer garden overlooking the traffic passing by on Whitegate Drive.

Forest Gate

You don't see many rowing boats going up and down Mere Road these days, but until drainage improvements were carried out by Blackpool Council in the 1960s that is exactly what used to happen.

Leaves from newly-planted trees which lined the roads were known to block gullies and cause flooding, especially in the low-lying Mere Road.

The junction of Mere Road with Forest Gate and the then-tram tracked Whitegate Drive is seen in

the 1920s in our first photograph and you can just make out a woman pushing a pram across Forest Gate.

The Whitegate Drive Baptist Church of 1910 stands in the centre, replaced in 1926 by a larger church on the corner of Forest Gate and Mere Road.

This once-proud ecclesiastical monument can be seen in the 1950s picture. Traffic lights have been installed at this increasingly busy junction and the 16B double-decker carries passengers from Wordsworth Avenue, via Stanley Park, back to Blackpool Central, according to its destination board.

The tram rails and wires of the Marton route can still be seen in the picture.

The church was bulldozed in 2001 because of costly structural problems and subsidence and the third of our photographs, shows the current street scene.

A block of 15 luxury apartments has replaced the setting of the church. The congregation has worshipped for three years in a new two-storey building behind, known as Forest Gate Baptist Church.

Waterloo Road

Now here's a sight you won't see these days – a white-gloved policeman, hand in the air, directing traffic at a Blackpool road junction.

The bobby is out there on the cobbles, ensuring good flow where Lytham Road and Waterloo Road cross. You might ask what happened to the motorists because they were not exactly plentiful when this scene was captured in the early 1920s.

In this view looking down Waterloo Road towards the Promenade is the Dog and

Partridge Hotel on the corner of Lytham Road. This old Boddington's pub was demolished in the late 1960s and a new one built a little further along Lytham Road.

The block of shops on the right, with the extensive poster advertising on the side, was also demolished around the same time to make way for a more modern row.

And when the original photograph was taken, who could have imagined that one day there would be a permanent police "presence" courtesy of the spying eye of the closed circuit TV camera on the pole outside the bakery.

Raikes Parade

Everything in the garden was lovely in the first of our two photographs of Raikes Parade at the corner of Church Street and Park Road.

Today, admittedly, there are a few flower beds left, much-admired no doubt by the vagrants who congregate on the benches. There is also a busy one-way road cutting through, a pelican crossing and a big expanse of pavement.

Taken in the early 1920s, the earlier photograph clear shows the entrance to

Raikes Hall Park or the Royal Palace gardens as it was otherwise known. The length of Church Street was known as Raikes Hill and the Grosvenor pub in the distance on the right – now part of an eyesore derelict block – was previously the Raikes Hotel. The small white building on the right, long-demolished, at one time housed the Raikes Smithy.

Foxhall Pub

Sir Thomas Tyldesley would doubtless be happy if he could see how things have turned out at his old Blackpool homestead.
He was a lad who liked a party and once wrote in his diary: "We drank the house drye."

That was in 1712 and, in recent times, successive generations of holidaymakers and locals alike have tried to follow the old squire's example at The Foxhall pub which stands on the site.

that admission was free "to the Harmonic Room open daily" and at which "the best of talent only engaged". To the left is the Circular Tour toast rack tramcar Number 72 heading back towards Talbot Square.

The second photograph shows the same pub in 1986 and the most recent picture features the current hostelry, still retaining the name The Foxhall which was opened in July 1991.

The original hall survived largely intact behind the hotel until the late 1860s. The earliest of these pictures dates from the 1920s.

At that time proprietor Leonard Seed advertised

Pleasant Street

Green Stripe Scotch whisky was obviously a favourite tipple, judging by the advertising hoarding on the side of a building in this 1920s view of Pleasant Street, North Shore, from the corner of Egerton Road.

At that time fields stretched inland from here to Layton with only scattered buildings. In the 19th century, Cliffe House and gardens stood to the right on the edge of the growing Blackpool. Part of the house remains today in Lynn

Grove, originally Cliffe Grove.

Since it was taken, the houses in Pleasant Street have developed into hotels and holiday flats, as can be seen by the new photograph.

And all those fields to Layton have long ago been built on.

Dickson Road

There's still a pub at the end of this street – but now it has a different name. Come to that, so has the road itself.

When the first photograph was taken, in about 1920, this was quiet Warbreck Road. Now we know the same stretch, viewed from the junction of Warley Road, as Dickson Road, North Shore.

The view is towards Gynn Square and at the bottom of the hill the gable end of the Duke of Cambridge Hotel is visible, prior to the building

of the present Gynn Hotel.

The picture shows houses interspersed by shops and the road is slowly changing into a shopping area to cater for the growing residential district.

Down the hill are double tram tracks but spaced too close together for trams to pass each other. This unusual situation was apparently known as a "double-single line".

In 1903 a passing point had been made which appears in the foreground.

Today's contrasting photograph shows that the gardens are long gone, as are the terraced buildings use as houses, gone over to shops.

However in the distance of both photographs the dome of the Savoy Hotel can be seen above the rooftops.

South Shore

Blackpool was first taking shape during the roaring twenties.

The resort appeared in a hurry after the First World War and massive developments included the opening of both the new South Promenade and Stanley Park, unveiled on the same day in 1926 by the Earl of Derby.

A four-year project had seen the promenade extended from the South Pier – then known as the Victoria Pier – up to the Lytham St Annes boundary. A series of decorative sunken gardens were created along

with a 25 foot wide footpath alongside the seawall, providing protection from the crashing waves.

Each of the gardens had a different character with features including lawn tennis courts, putting green, even a rock garden with a stream of water which emerged from a weeping cave. The central feature at Harrowside was a yachting pond for children surrounded by shelters and colonnade.

But the new millennium saw a new, and far more controversial, lease of life for the South Shore seafront with the arrival of the Great Promenade Show – 12 works of public art, some of them six metres high. They included the Mirrorball, an abstract spiky sculpture called Desire and the High Tide Organ.

The ambitious outdoor gallery scheme was given pride of place on the newly-rebuilt £20m seafront where sea defences had been transformed, combining a robust barrier to flooding with an elegant landscaped walkway on two levels.

Modern shelters were erected, a dazzling solar-powered lighting system installed and 16 circular sites along a two kilometre stretch became mini-amphitheatres for the public artworks which invoked both criticism and praise when first installed in 2001.

Queens Promenade

Here's a seafront building that is literally at the Cliffs edge – but in no danger of falling into the sea.

Back in 1922, in the earlier of these pictures, the property was the isolated Brynn Tivy Hotel on Queens Promenade.

By 1937, the seafront hotel had been greatly extended, modernised and refurbished to occupy the present block between King Edward Avenue and Empress Drive.

Today the former Brynn Tivy is the southern corner

of the well-known Cliffs,
owned by the resort's largest
family-run and owned hotel
group, Choice, whose
empire also takes in the
Claremont and Viking, as
well as two properties in the
Lake District.

Bunnock Hall

At Hoo Hill, near the Windmill Hotel, Little Layton, the lanes from Bispham and Poulton converged by an old cottage, with a corrugated iron roof.

The cottage, demolished in 1923, was at the junction of Bispham and Poulton roads and had been there for well over 100 years, previously having had a thatched roof.

During the 1800s it was known as Bunnock Hall but later became known as Dick Blackburn's cottage. Dick was a gravedigger. Outside

the cottage at the corner of the wall was a stone which was a favourite resting place for those travelling between Blackpool and Poulton or Bispham.

Behind Bunnock Hall, a little way down Poulton Road, was Hoo Hill farm which came into being in the 1840s. Henry Fisher had bought the land from William Gratrix and then Thomas Strickland became tenant farmer.

By the end of the century it was being farmed by the Pye brothers George and John. Their parents and their other brothers were at Ingthorpe Grange, Bispham. The family had come from the Wyresdale area. The farm was knocked down in the late 1920s when the Nickson family, who then owned it, sold it for development.

The above photograph looks east towards Wade's Farm, Little Carleton, and shows the new Poulton Road under construction. The third photograph gives an up-to-date view of where the cottage stood.

Golden Mile

The southern end of the Golden Mile.

To the right of our first photograph, taken in 1925, is Fairyland.

The first property on this site was a bathing house and later a hotel known as Wylies South Pier Hotel before it was demolished at the turn of the last century.

The neo-classical building in the centre, clad in white faience, was built by Albert Lindsay Parkinson, with Tom G Lumb as architect. It included a large café area, hall and shops

and was ready to be let in March 1913.

Over the years the picture house was known variously as Central Beach Cinema, Trocadero and, before it closed for good in 1971, The Ritz.

Fairyland included a scenic ride and a roller skating room upstairs but by the 1960s – as the later picture shows – the ground floor had been taken over by coin-operated amusement machines.

The 1970 redevelopment and widening of the Chapel Street junction meant the closure and demolition of this Golden Mile landmark, although the latest picture, shows that almost a century on, there is still a place for a distinctive building at the end of a row of modern arcades.

Sandcastle/ South Shore Open Air Pool

The South Shore outdoor swim pool, built at a cost of £70,000 officially opened in 1923 when the resort was fast becoming the place to be with two million visitors in one week alone.

Built for those visitors of hardier days who did not mind swimming in cold temperatures, the Open Air

Baths was said to have been modelled on the Colosseum of Rome.

Over the years it provided a catwalk for hundreds of would-be bathing beauty queens, judged by the resort's summer show stars.

In the early 30s it became a backdrop for the film *Sing As We Go*, starring Gracie Fields and in 1959 another movie star, Hollywood's Jayne Mansfield visited when she came to switch on Blackpool Illuminations.

But the picture had changed by the mid-sixties. The bath was now a white elephant according to many and over the coming years there were various proposals from a sports stadium to pop concert venue, a killer whale show, even an ornate angling pool stocked with trout.

The bulldozers arrived in February 1983 reducing the site to rubble in just five weeks. It was to be replaced by the £16 million Sandcastle Waterpark.

As well as a tropical swim centre, the Sandcastle contained a huge entertainment hall and night spot – now a Casino – designed to keep the visitors happy whatever the hour and rain or shine.

Gynn Square

The first of the two pictures dates from the late 1920s when new safety crossings, painted yellow with white borders, were being provided at the Gynn junction.

Workmen can be seen painting the words Cross Here and while three people are using the new shaded area to safely cross Warbreck Hill Road, as many again are about to take their chances just yards away.

There was no roundabout in those days, but as the accompanying

caption told readers: "There are many complicated lines of traffic."

The same type of crossing was later extended to other busy parts of the resort. The Sunken Gardens – or Jubilee Gardens as it is known now after a tidy up –

can be seen in both pictures, although the two Colonnades are hidden by the modern tram shelter in this photograph.

Stanley Park

Stanley Park was named after the famous Lancashire family the Stanley's and was officially opened by the-then head of the dynasty, the 17th Earl of Derby on October 2, 1926.

The land was previously a collection of hen runs, pigsties and stagnant ponds and more than half the park's 250 acres were bought by Sir Lindsay Parkinson for 4.5d (about 2p) a year freehold and turned over to the Corporation at the same price.

The new lodges and entrance gates at the east end of Mere Road are seen in the first picture leading the visitors up the newly planted drive into the park.

Cocker Clock Tower

Not before time... the Cocker Memorial Clock Tower in Blackpool's Stanley Park has been restored.

The earlier of the two photographs dates from 1927, the year when the memorial was officially opened by Alderman Sir John Bickerstaffe in honour of Alderman William Henry Cocker (1836 to 1911).

In the distance you can clearly see not only Blackpool Tower, but the Big Wheel that sat where the Olympia is today.

Dr Cocker was the eldest son of Dr John Cocker and practised in Blackpool up to

1875 before devoting his time to public and private interests and in 1876 he became the first Mayor and Freeman of Blackpool.

He sold his house – Bank Hey – at the top of Victoria Street to the Winter Gardens Company in 1875 for £23,000 and owned much of the town centre's land. His philosophy was that money was there to be used, and he spent much on entertaining – most famously when he picked up the tab for the lavish banquet held for the Lord Mayor of London and mayors of 68 towns at the opening of the Winter Gardens in 1878.

Yet, it is said, he died a poor and lonely man, living in a modest house on Whitegate Drive.

The later photograph shows the tower after its much-needed clean-up in 2006.

Church Street

The distinctive dome on the roof of the Winter Gardens is now masked to shoppers in Church Street by the modern block of shops at the junction with Coronation Street.

The complex is, in fact, a cunning late 1990s re-modelling of a former Littlewoods department store, which once housed the resort's tax office on upper floors.

In the earlier photograph, the white building between the Winter Gardens and the shops was the Adelphi

Hotel, which even had its own balcony overlooking Church Street.

On the opposite side of Coronation Street, the property which is now a jewellers, was once the site of one of Blackpool's earliest post offices.

Highfield Road

Highfield Road, South Shore, as seen in the 1930s from a position on the south side of the road at the junction with Lytham Road.

The left corner, which seems empty, was St Mary's Church, which later relocated to a new building in Mayfield Avenue.

St James' Road, whilst accessible via a footpath, was not yet a road access from Highfield Road.

In 1932 the owners of the first few shops on the right were C.L. Ainsworth selling

sweets & tobacco;
F.Harbron, grocer; A.&
F.Dixon, drapers; Lewis &
Lockwood, cycle agents;
Joseph Birtwistle, plumbers
and hardware; and the last
shop, clearly visible on the
corner with Mayfield
Avenue, was Dawson's

Drapers, shortly afterwards
renamed Byers.

Palatine Hotel

The Tower is still standing, but what of the other buildings in the first of these two photographs, taken around 1930.

The Palatine (Family and Commercial) Hotel stood on the Promenade corner of Hounds Hill opposite Central Station.

It advertised in the 1907 Blackpool Official Guide under the management of Mr H. Powell Jones as being newly decorated and refurnished.

It also had electric lights, hot, cold and sea water baths, "large and well-lighted" stockroom, excellent cuisine, table d'hote served at separate tables and was a free house.

Prior to the hotel being built, a row of houses named Queens Terrace, built in 1848, stood along there. Progress struck again in the

1970s when the Palatine was demolished and replaced by a complex of shops, amusements and nightspots.

At the same time a modern concrete bridge was erected across the Promenade, with access by escalators which very quickly broke down and rusted up thanks to the salt air.

Stanley Terrace – Midland Bank

The first of our three photographs, taken in 1934, shows the demolition of Stanley Terrace for road widening, later replaced with the Art Deco style block still known today as Stanley Buildings. The second picture from 1954, shows the tramlines of the Marton route.

Today the Midland Bank building has become a late night takeaway and where traffic once crossed between Church Street and Caunce Street, Blackpool, there is now a large expanse of

pavement. In the distance, the former Regent Cinema, later offering bingo, is a snooker hall.

Corporation Street

The first of these two photographs brings a whole new meaning to the word horsepower.

Faithful beasts were brought into Blackpool town centre to play an integral role in clearing the snow back in the late 1920s.

Two carts are fully laden on Corporation Street close to the junction with West Street and, in the distance, the Town Hall still boasts its distinctive spire. The original St John's Market can be seen to the right of the photograph.

The building housing the Orient Café later became a Boots store, and was destroyed by fire in 1936. Two years later the present building was opened with a Boots store in the basement and ground floor and municipal offices above.

Today it houses Blackpool Council's Customer First centre.

Birley Street

Where do we park in Blackpool town centre – and for how long?

That's the question on the lips of many motorists today as they inevitably play a cat and mouse game with the resort's army of traffic wardens.

But, as the earlier of these two photographs shows, on-street parking was very much a problem back in the mid-1930s.

Birley Street, seen here looking down to Market Street long before pedestrianisation was a

council byword, was bumper
to bumper with cars.

Ivy House Cottage

In 1935 Fred and Bertha Wood purchased a rundown three acre nursery and the 19th century cobblestone Ivy House Cottage on the east side of Common Edge Road, Marton Moss.

Unable to earn a living from the nursery they obtained a licence for a permanent campsite. The new camp was, appropriately, called Ivy House Holiday Camp. With chalet accommodation for 135 campers, it became a huge success during the 1950s and 1960s, becoming Marton Moss's very own Hi De Hi holiday camp.

During the Second World War the camp was commandeered by the Army and RAF and it also accommodated wartime evacuees.

In the mid 1960s Fred and Bertha sold the holiday camp and by the late 1980s the site had fallen into disrepair and was subsequently demolished.

The photograph of Ivy House Cottage dates from the mid-1950s and the second picture shows the site today which is now luxury housing in the shape of Belverdale Gardens.

Savoy Café

It was all change in the late 1930s on this northerly stretch of Central Promenade.

The focus is on the block between West Street and Church Street and the first of the pictures, taken 70 years ago, shows demolition in progress.

The black and white building, dating back to 1835, was torn down in 1937 to make way for what was described on its opening the following year as "a strikingly modern, almost ultra-modern structure that must rank among the best of Blackpool's architectural

achievements". Like its predecessor had done for some 23 years, the new property also housed the prestigious Savoy Café – this time boasting four storeys.

Today the complex contains Brannigans and a bowling complex.

Then, as now, Roberts Oyster Bar, far left on each photograph, was a popular haunt for those seeking seafood.

And while the timber clad Savoy was long ago reduced to rubble, still intact – for the time being, at least – is the three storey terracotta building sandwiched between there and the Oyster Rooms.

In 1937, the ground floor was Richardson's chemists, with the upper rooms to let. Today it is a gift shop although there are plans to redevelop the site.

Church Street

Five old cottages are demolished in Church Street in 1937 to make way for a new and ultra modern garage.

The wall, railings and tidy privet hedge might have gone from the property to the right of the cottages. Yet that same building, somewhat remodelled, remains today, as does the three-storey block at the other side, now with an extra window at first floor level.

The original Raikes Garage (top right) opened in 1938 and later became T H Bennett.

The petrol pumps went some years ago, followed by the top of the range cars

that gleamed inside the Mercedes Benz showrooms. Founder Tom Bennett, a keen racehorse owner, died, aged 93, in November 2003, leaving £4.5 million to 16 charities – a dozen of them relating to animals, from dogs to donkeys.

Today the premises, bathed in a distinctive green, is the home of Easthams solicitors.

Dominion Cinema

How many shoppers in Red Bank Road, Bispham can remember the last picture show at the long-demolished Dominion Cinema?

Plans were drawn up in 1935 for a seating capacity of 1,634 plus a cabaret café and a dance floor for 200 people.

It took a mere seven weeks to construct and was opened in June 1938 by MP Roland Robinson (who at that time was campaigning for holidays with pay), boasting "equipment which

will permit the incorporation of TV programmes immediately they become practical in this part of the country".

Among those who appeared there was comedian Alex Munro, whose daughter was to become the screen actress Janet Munro.

The Dominion closed on September 15, 1962, having shown El Cid as its last film. The property was bought by a Leeds firm, demolished, and the site used as a car park for four years until redeveloped as shops.

Preston New Road

Today this is one of Blackpool's busiest junctions.

Despite the sophisticated traffic management system, motorists heading in and out of the resort at peak times are still likely to find themselves gridlocked in Oxford Square, Marton, frustrated as they end up in lengthy queues from Waterloo Road, Park Road, Whitegate Drive and Preston New Road. It wasn't always so, as this picture, dating back to the Second World War, shows.

Passengers have almost filled the old style tram bound for Royal Oak and a lone cyclist passes in the opposite direction at the start of Waterloo Road.

Allotments at the edge of Whitegate Drive remain today, but long gone are the air raid shelters, surrounded by railings, on the islands.

Solarium

It was in 1938 that work began on the new £9,000 'Winter Gardens' for South Promenade, South Shore, but the name was later changed to the Harrowside Sun Parlours.

From dawn to dusk the sun parlour attracted visitors in their hundreds not least because it served as an antidote to the frantic pace of the Pleasure Beach and Golden Mile.

The pity is that no one had the foresight to preserve that popularity or maintain the building – or the precious plants within. It fell on hard times after years of neglect. Various dedicated locals had a go at keeping it going but the dilapidated building finally became a boarded up target for vandals.

Hoteliers and locals united in 1999 behind a bid to win lottery funding to restore it to its former glory and make it an arts, crafts and community centre.

They got the campaign rolling but missed out on

the cash – but happily vital funds have since seen the building transformed as part of a multi-agency project with includes Blackpool Council, Blackpool Challenge Partnership, North West Development Agency and the New Opportunity Fund.

The £1.8 million Solaris today is a centre for environmental excellence – with community rooms and training units, exhibition areas and community café to be used as a valuable resource by schools, the local community and visitors.

With cutting-edge technology at the heart of the project, the Solaris opened in November 2004 and is totally self sufficient, which means it can generate its own heat and light – through solar panels and two eye-catching wind turbines on its frontage.

Grand Theatre

The Grand Theatre, pictured here in the 1940s, was originally opened in 1894. Yet Matcham's architectural masterpiece came close to meeting the same fate as Feldman's and the Palace.

A plan to demolish the theatre first reared its ugly head in the summer of 1972. A campaign launched by theatregoers, who later became known as the Friends of the Grand, caused sufficient concern to force a public inquiry at which the theatre won a reprieve.

By then the theatre had become a Grade II listed building. But the theatre failed to reopen and became derelict. It did open in 1977 – but as a bingo hall.

The Friends succeeded in saving the Grand by raising the necessary funds – with the help of Blackpool Council, the Arts Council and Lancashire County Council – to purchase the theatre from owners EMI in September 1980.

Chesterfield Road

Whatever happened to all those corner shops that were once a vital part of our everyday life?

That's the question posed by Heather Ennis (née Brown), whose late parents Frank and Joyce used to run such an establishment in Blackpool in the early 1970s.

Heather, who now lives in Ponteland, Northumberland, says: "We had a shop at the corner of Chesterfield Road and Sherbourne Road, North Shore and it was always full.

"In those days as well as Claremont Primary School around the corner there was also Claremont Girls and we

did a roaring trade in home made ice lollies."

The picture postcard of the property dates from the late 1940s – when the owner was also offering accommodation to holidaymakers. When Heather grew up there, those bedrooms housed the family.

On the reverse of the card it boasts that a Mrs Campbell offered "apartments or board residence, hot and cold water, terms moderate" at what was known as Dalkeith House.

The hand painted sign in the window said

"Campbells high class groceries and provisions" and there were advertisements for Robinson's Bread, Players Bachelor cigarettes, Oxydol, Fairy Soap, Turog bread and the splendidly-named Shinio.

There is a wooden phone box at the edge of the property, later replaced by the once-familiar red version.

As the second of our pictures shows, the property

still stands, but passers-by, who probably make most of their purchases at one of the many superstores across the Fylde coast, would never know there had been a shop or boarding house.

There's a patio door where the shop windows once were and although the gateposts remain, the brick wall has been extended and the home painted, rendered and modernised.

Pleasure Beach

Whether it is the wooden tracks of the Big Dipper or the steel tubes of The Big One – thrill seekers have always found more than their share of fun at the country's busiest tourist attraction, Pleasure Beach in Blackpool.

This seafront collection of rides, attractions, shows and stalls, has been wowing the crowds for more than 100 years.

And in these days of corporate holdings, it is refreshing that here is one business that remains firmly in family hands – the fourth generation of the Thompson family.

Each year, the fun park brings in the latest attractions yet retains many of the old favourites.

Lindsay Avenue

Looking south along Whitegate Drive towards Marton.

The first picture dates back to just after the Second World War and captures the street scene from the junction with Lindsay Avenue to beyond Airedale Avenue. The later photograph (top right) from 1952, roughly taken from the same spot, but this time capturing the tramsheds and the Saddle pub.

Our up to date picture focuses on the entire stretch seen in both the earlier

ones. Gone are the tramsheds, replaced by a petrol station, and the Saddle, still a popular watering hole, has lost the boarding around the roof.

County Hotel

It was declared the end of an era when the seafront Palace was demolished in the 1960s to make way for another form of entertainment – shopping.

The short stretch of Central Promenade that it occupied had long been Blackpool's most desirable building site. Hotels, houses, even bath-houses were developed there over the 18th and 19th centuries.

But the area came into its own with the advent of theatre.

First the Prince of Wales Theatre. Then the sumptuously ornate

Alhambra, out to rival the Tower. Later, under a Tower Company buyout, the Palace Varieties, known as the People's Popular Palace of Pleasure.

The Palace – variety hall, theatre, ballroom, erstwhile circus, skating rink and picture house – was demolished in 1961.

You can just see the end of the Palace's glass canopy on the right of the picture. Yet there was another building on that site – the neighbouring County Hotel, built in 1866.

The whole site was demolished to make way for Lewis's, Blackpool's last, since lost, "proper" department store. The flagship store, with its distinctive modernist architecture and sea-green honeycomb panelled frontage, had become a

landmark even as the doors opened to a crowd of 1,500 shoppers, in April, 1964.

Lewis's closed in January 1993 and Woolworth's unveiled a £3m plan for a new store, which meant demolishing the upper floors of the existing building and remodelling the exterior.

Today it is also home to other smaller store units, a "mothballed" Mecca Bingo hall and a Harry Ramsden's fish and chips "with chandeliers" restaurant.

Princess Cinema

The last picture show at the Princess Cinema was in 1981 – the end of a 69 year era for Blackpool's second oldest purpose-built movie house.

EMI sold off the North Promenade building following the conversion of the ABC Cinema in Church Street (which it also owned) into a three-studio complex.

Today, both properties are enjoying new leases of life as successful nightspots: the Princess as Club Sanuk and the ABC as The Syndicate.

The Princess gained its

name on account of a visit to Blackpool by Princess Marie Louise to open nearby Princess Parade.

It was opened in 1912 on the site of a funfair and roller-skating rink, enlarged and re-opened in 1922 and re-modernised in 1937.

When the older picture was taken in 1952, Scaramouche, starring Stewart Granger and Janet Leigh, was the featured film.

1950s-1960s

Mereside Estate

It's not every council house tenant who has an historic windmill for a neighbour.

But the Mereside estate, which welcomed its first residents in 1949, developed alongside Little Marton Mill – a familiar sight to millions of holidaymakers making their way in and out of Blackpool along Preston New Road.

The listed building was given to Blackpool Council by Cornelius Bagot, as a memorial to the late Allen Clarke – author, historian,

leading dialect writer and *Gazette* journalist.

The mill, dating back to 1838, still stands in an open space on the estate, which was given street names drawn from the map of the Lake District.

The view is along Langdale Road and, in the older picture, taken in 1952, the Co-op milkman had already built up a round of deliveries for the daily pint. After all, this was long before the days of one-stop superstore shopping.

Clifton Road, bordering part of the estate, was then a narrow, single-track route, with a dyke at either side.

And Marton itself has a much more rural feel with several farms sited around the Mereside fringes.

Bus Station

Blackpool has bustled with buses ever since charabancs and trains brought the first trippers to Britain's number one holiday resort.

Here buses pack the Talbot Mews traffic park, alongside the Blackpool North rail station, in 1932.

The pavements are crowded with visitors burdened by heavy luggage moving too and from their hotels and guesthouses.

Nine years later the bus station and four-storey car park opened - and was hailed as one of

Blackpool's outstanding buildings. The imposing multi-storey, which cost £162,152 was 80 foot tall and could hold more than 1,000 cars. Its original cream and green terracotta exterior displayed multi-coloured panels depicting progress in transport. It was reclad in the 1960s when the tiles were considered to be in an unsafe condition.

In 2006 the bus station was earmarked for demolition as part of the £227m redevelopment of the Talbot Gateway project to revitalise the area.

Derby Baths

Now you see it, now you don't!

Where today there is just grass next to the Hilton Hotel on North Promenade, once there was the imposing Derby Baths.

Blackpool's civic fathers paid tribute to the then Lord Derby, by naming the town's new Olympic-sized swimming pool after him.

Derby Baths cost £270,000 to build but the outbreak of war meant Lord Derby was unable to perform the official opening ceremony in May 1940 as

planned. This photograph was taken in 1953.

However, his grandson was able to do the honours when the neighbouring sauna centre opened in 1965. The loss-making baths' complex was demolished amid much controversy towards the end of Conservative control of Blackpool Council in 1990.

Coronation Street

To the casual eye, the structure above Coronation Street might resemble a cable car, making its way back to the seafront, almost a stone's throw away.

But then things are not always what they seem.

The box was, in fact, a familiar sight in Blackpool at one time – a distinctive street light strung above every major road junction, in this case where Hornby Road crosses Coronation Street, in 1953

The box displayed red glazing to motorists on the

major roads and amber on the minor roads. Traffic was obviously so light in times past that this was sufficient to warn visitors of a hazardous cross road.

In the distance on the right is the distinctive white tiled corner entrance to the Olympia Hall of the Winter Gardens.

Abbatoir Road

What's in a name? Quite a lot, apparently, if you are building a housing development and are keen to change an image.

Which is presumably why Abbatoir Road in Blackpool changed overnight into...Coopers Way.

With a slaughterhouse at the end of the cul-de-sac, the original name was obviously felt appropriate by the town's planners in decades past.

But then Coopers Way is equally appropriate as the estate, close to the Talbot

Road junction, was built on the site of the abbatoir's neighbour, the Catterall and Swarbrick's Queens Brewery.

The company also owned a string of pubs in Blackpool and the Fylde and sold their XL ales and best mild to many other outlets – before takeovers by United Breweries, Charrington and Bass.

And here's a sobering thought – the last mild brewed in Abbatoir Road in the early 1970s cost just 1s 9d (9p) a pint...

Bloomfield Road

Oh be joyful. Blackpool Football Club's packed ground photographed from the air in the halcyon days of the 1950s when the Seasiders were a top First Division outfit.

The rooftops of the west and east stands are blazoned with advertising for Dutton's beers and ... Premier Garage.

The stands were packed during an era when the Seasiders reached Wembley finals – losing 4-2 to Manchester United in 1948 and 2-0 to Newcastle United in 1951 – before triumphing in the "Matthews" final of 1953.

Blackpool's 4-3 win over

Bolton is still regarded as one of the greatest sporting comebacks of all time, but while wing wizard Stanley Matthews was regarded as the hero – Stanley Mortensen grabbed the three goals which, to this day, makes him the only player ever to have scored a hat trick in an FA Cup final at Wembley.

In contrast the latest aerial view shows the new two-sided stadium. The North and West sides of the ground were redeveloped at the cost of £7 million and opened in February 2002. Work is due to start at a later date on the construction of the South Stand running alongside Bloomfield Road which will be named after Seasiders' legend Jimmy Armfield.

And Oh be joyful could be the cry today after Blackpool's 2-0 Wembley win over Yeovil to earn a place in soccer's second tier for the first time in over 30 years.

Tower Ballroom

Take your partners please... Blackpool's magnificent Tower Ballroom has always been a firm favourite with dancers of all ages, as well as those who simply come to admire the architecture or savour the atmosphere with a few hours away from everything amid the ornate surroundings.

It was a different story in 1956 when a carelessly discarded cigarette end resulted in an inferno that took hold beneath the floor and crept almost the entire length of the ballroom, flames breaking free in one area, leaping three feet into the air.

At one point the ballroom was under four inches of water and it still wasn't enough to douse the blaze. Firemen hacked through the floor to release hundreds of gallons of water – and this overflow cascaded down the steps of the stairs on the approach to the ballroom and flooded the main entrance.

Fortunately, tarpaulin had been placed over the ballroom's famous Wurlizter organ to save it from damage.

The Gazette reported a scene of "desolation and destruction, a grim waste of smoke, running water, char-red wood and fire hoses."

Cost of repair was put at £250,000 and within three years the Tower had a brand new look, while the ballroom itself was restored to its former glory, gold leaf and all.

70-year-old Andrew Mazzei, who had worked in the ballroom as a boy, and whose father had worked on the original design, rose to the tremendous challenge. He had made a name designing sets for some of the biggest British films and spent weeks studying the ruined decor from floor to floor, using original photographs as his guide.

South Pier

Today the entrance to South Pier has circus-style stripes – in keeping with the candyfloss and funfair trappings. The theatre is long gone, replaced by an end-of-pier rollercoaster.

Back in the 1960s, when the first of these pictures was taken, the arcade was known as The Beachcomber and the theatre, which had replaced the Grand Pavilion, destroyed by fire in 1958, had a wide range of entertainment.

There was everything from the Sooty Show to

international wrestling, while
the main summer show
boasted the likes of Eden
Kane, the Karl Denver Trio
and Marty Wilde.

Hippodrome

There has been entertainment on this site in Church Street, Blackpool, for at least 112 years.

The building itself dates back to 1895 as the Empire Theatre and Opera House.

It was renamed the Hippodrome, after conversion into a circus, in 1900, with further work in 1910 when it became a cinema.

The building, pictured in 1961, closed the following year. The auditorium was virtually demolished, except for the outer walls, before it

re-opened in May 1963 as the ABC Theatre, with summer shows and a winter cinema.

Converted into a triple cinema in 1981 it changed its name at the end of the decade to Cannon, then became the MGM and finally reverted to ABC before the very last picture show in July 2000.

For the first time in 40 years, old brickwork, including a series of distinctive arches, was on view to Blackpool shoppers in summer 2002 as our picture (above) shows.

Workmen had removed cladding on the property while working on the exterior facelift for the new lease of life as the Syndicate super club that December.

Now under new ownership, The Syndicate re-opened in 2006 after a much-publicised closure that involved licensing wrangles.

Talbot Hotel

The success of crown green bowling in Blackpool was an offshoot of the resort being a favourite holiday town for Lancashire miners.

While the wives and children spent their time at various entertainment spots or on the beach, the men played crown bowls on the green at the rear of the Talbot Hotel.

This popular hostelry, owned by Blackpool brewery Catterall and Swarbrick, was at the junction of Talbot Road and Topping Street.

Traffic at the busy

junction was controlled for years by a point duty policeman, as shown in our 1966 picture, before the present traffic flow system and traffic lights were introduced.

The pub was demolished two years later to make way for Prudential House, an office block with shops and a supermarket at ground level. There was also an extension to the adjacent Talbot Road multi-storey car park with space for an additional 112 cars.

R H O Hills

Blackpool's flagship department store for many decades was RHO Hills, which first opened as a one-storey novelty bazaar in Bank Hey Street in 1884.

Forty years later a Mr W Vyner took over the bazaar, demolished it and pioneered a four-storey building on the same site. It certainly was an impressive building in Bank Hey Street when it reopened in

modern guise in 1968, as our picture shows, following a major blaze.

The £1.5m fire, which blasted through the heart of Blackpool town centre in May 1967 was the second time the store, just behind the Tower, had been burned out.

The previous blaze came in 1932 when the store was full of customers and staff but there was no panic and everyone got out safely.

The 1967 outbreak was discovered early in the morning and within a couple of hours, the five-storey building had been reduced to a smoking ruin. At the height of the blaze, firefighters on turntable ladders tackled the flames which leapt 100 feet into the sky.

Hills eventually changed its name to Binns having been taken over by the giant House of Fraser Group in 1975, but the store closed down in November 1987.

Later incarnations have seen the store re-emerge as the Tower Shopping Centre, then Littlewoods, from 1995-2005, and more recently as a Primark department store.

Miner's Home

SELDOM has the Prince of Wales, for all his worldwide popularity, had a reception of more homely and hearty enthusiasm. So reported *The Gazette* back in 1927 when Edward passed through an almost unbroken avenue of cheering residents and holidaymakers along nine miles ofcoast from Lytham to Bispham.

He was here, on June 28, to open the Lancashire and Cheshire Miners Convalescent Home on Queens Promenade.

After waving to the throng of people, Edward, accompanied by Lord Derby

and other dignitaries, went to the main entrance door, which he opened with a golden key, presented to the Prince in a casket by the architect.

The Prince then entered the building, followed by more than 100 guests, and signed the first entry in the visitors book with the signature Edward P.

For decades the home provided a place where miners could recuperate from illness brought on by the harsh conditions in which they worked.

The property continued to operate as a convalescent home for miners until the late 1980s when it became something of a forgotten landmark.

Now, as Admiral Point, it has been restored and converted into apartments, flanked by two modern blocks with further homes at the rear of the site.

CONTRIBUTOR PAGES

Chris & Kathy Arkwright
Kirk Atkinson
Ken Bailie
John Barrow
John Baxter
John Beardow
Gerald Beesley
Professor and Mrs P Beighton
Mr Peter Benson
Mr Jack Bentham
Elizabeth Beswick
Stuart Bimpson
Kevan Bishop
David John Bonney
Mr & Mrs B Bradshaw
Melvin Brandon
Sheila Scott Broadbent
James Cecil Brown
Trevor Burrows
Mr Granville Carr
Frank Cartmell
Angela Champion
Fred Champion
Mr Reg Cobb
B Collinge
John Terence Cooper
Adele Cottam
Mrs M Court
Mrs Joan Croft
Mr & Mrs G K Crook
Duncan John Crosby

Jake Cuthbertson
David Cyster
Jean Davies
Pat Deakin
Ronald Dean
Robert Charles Dewhirst
Emily Dickson
Hannah Dickson
Pat Dimuantes
Robin & Beryl Donnelly
Anne Douglas
Ronald Duke
Mrs S Duke
Elsie Eastwood
Harold Eastwood
Victoria Eaves
Rita Elliott
Miss Justine Ellis
Margaret Evans
Peter & Janet Fenton
Carol & Peter Ford
Elsie May Fricker
Jennie Isabel Gammon
Robert & Jeanne Goodrick
Nellie Gray
Richard Greenhalgh
Renee Greenwood
Mrs Yvonne Gregitis
Joyce Gregory
John Russell Hague
Peter S Hardman

Derek Hartley

Chris Hemingway

Mr E N Hey

Mr Raymond Hibberd

Barbara Hilton

Harold Stewart Hodgson

Edna Hodson nee Shaw

Brian Hornby

Mr Derek F Hoyle

Margaret Hunter

James Jackson

Kenneth Jackson

Janet James

Mrs Maisie Johnson

Peter & Tina Kenniford

Frank Kirby

Ken Kitching

Phyllis L Lamont

Denis Seymour Lane

Ms C Leigh-Baker

Peter Lever

David Liversidge

Colin Edwin MacLeod

Alex Maitland

Mrs Joan Marchant

Marie Marshall

John Massey

Jim & Alice McGowan

Ted McKinn

Mr Frank Metcalfe

Jack & Gillian Morgan

Colin Moxley

Rebecca Fleming Neal

Brian & Irene Neish

Keith J Nicholson

Nick Oakley

Robert Perry

Mr & Mrs D Potter

Jacqueline Victoria Pratt

Phillip Private

Laura Quigley

Andrew Robinson

Elsie Sadek

Eileen Sanday

Margaret A Sanderson

Sam Sanderson

Colin Shaw

Stephen Shepherd

Tony Shepherd

Mark Singleton

Mrs Betty Smith

Norma Somerside

Mark Spedding

Scott Stevens

Zoe Jayne Stevens

Keith Studd

Ethel Taylor nee Charlesworth

Mrs Gladys Threlfall

Peter Thurston Armstrong

Mr Philip Walsh

Mark Warburton

Anne-Marie Welding

Shaun Whiteley

Anthony Wood

Pauline Ann Wood

Neville R Woods

Malcolm Woof

Randall Wright